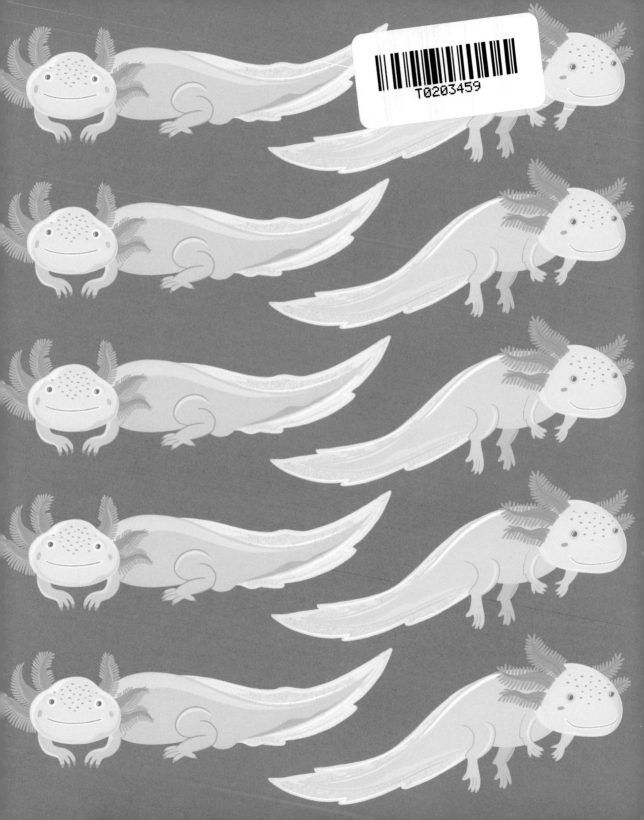

YOUNG ZOOLOGIST
AXOLOTL

A FIRST FIELD GUIDE TO THE AMPHIBIAN THAT NEVER GROWS UP

NEON SQUID

CONTENTS

4 Hello, young zoologist!

6 Before you get started

8 Meet the axolotl

10 Mutants

12 The family

14 A day in the life

16 Life cycle

18 Dance of the axolotls

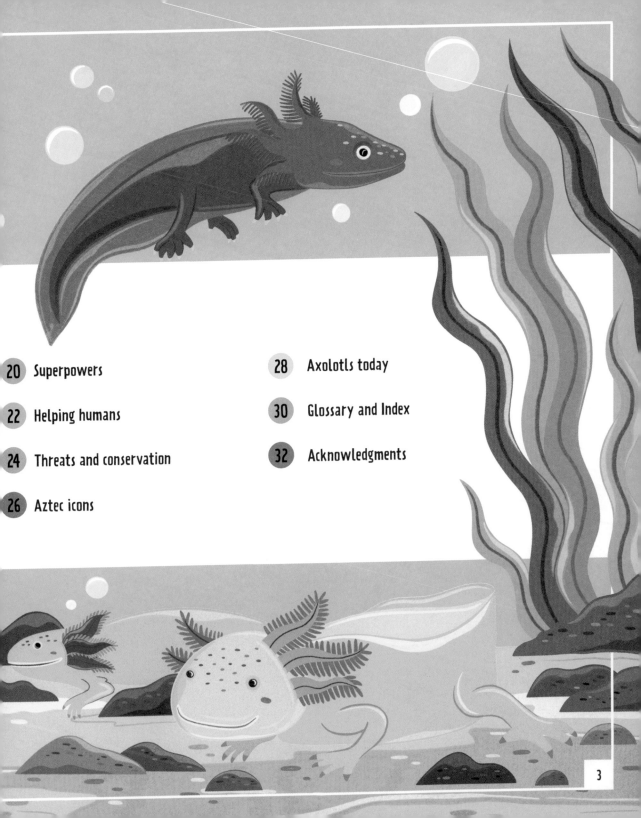

20 Superpowers

22 Helping humans

24 Threats and conservation

26 Aztec icons

28 Axolotls today

30 Glossary and Index

32 Acknowledgments

HELLO, YOUNG ZOOLOGIST!

My name is Jessica Whited. I've been fascinated by the natural world since I was a little kid like you, playing in the woods, fields, and streams. When I grew up, I decided to become a biologist so I could study amazing creatures every day. In my lab at Harvard University, Massachusetts, we explore how axolotls can do very cool things that we can't—like grow back their limbs! Let's have some fun learning about these mysterious animals and maybe you'll be inspired to crack their secrets, too...

DR. JESSICA LAMAE WHITED

FACT FILE

SCIENTIFIC NAME
Ambystoma mexicanum

CLASS
Amphibian

ORDER
Salamanders

FAMILY
Ambystomatidae

SIZE COMPARISON

WHERE THEY LIVE
Lake Xochimilco and Lake Chalco in Mexico

EATS

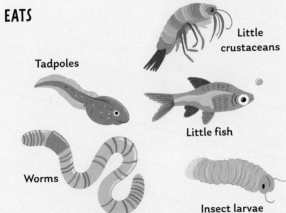

Little crustaceans

Tadpoles

Little fish

Worms

Insect larvae

WEIGHT
0.0004–0.5 lb (0.2–230 g)

HABITAT
Shallow, swampy lakes

CONSERVATION STATUS
Critically endangered

BEFORE YOU GET STARTED

1 **NOTEBOOK, PEN, AND PENCIL**

Be sure to bring a lab notebook so you can take careful notes, and don't forget a pencil and a pen! Good science requires precise documentation.

2 **BUG SPRAY**

The axolotl habitat can be pretty swampy, which is perfect for breeding mosquitos—tasty for axolotls, but annoying for us! It's essential to pack some insect repellent.

3 **SUNSCREEN**

Working outside in the hot sun can be hard work. If you're not careful you might burn. You'll want to slather on some sunscreen to protect your skin.

If you want to study these critters out in Lake Xochimilco and Lake Chalco, I hope you've brought all of your gear! Getting up close and personal with axolotls is easier in the lab, where they can be bred and raised in captivity.

4 MICROSCOPE
Using a microscope in a lab means you can see parts of an axolotl you wouldn't be able to with your naked eye. Microscopes can reveal details you could otherwise only imagine!

5 CAMERA
You can bring a camera on expeditions or hook it up to a microscope in the lab and make a permanent record of what you see to show your friends and colleagues.

6 COMPUTER
A computer will come in handy for analyzing things like axolotl DNA. It will also help you keep track of all your data, communicate with your colleagues, and read and write scientific articles.

MEET THE AXOLOTL

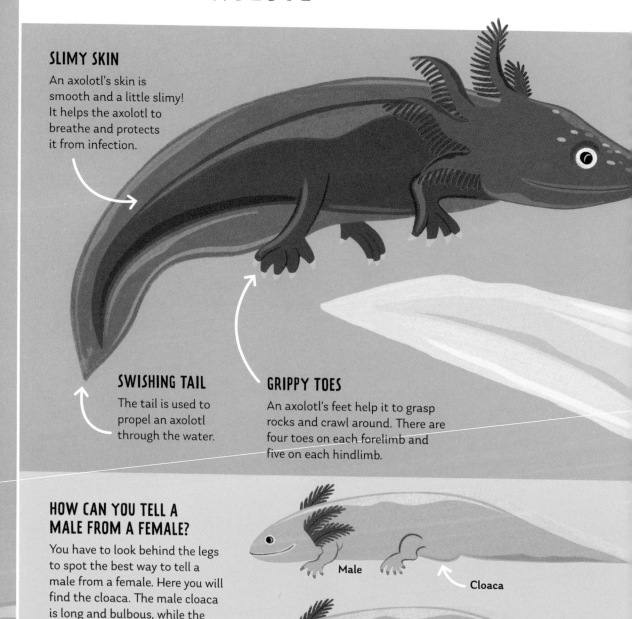

SLIMY SKIN

An axolotl's skin is smooth and a little slimy! It helps the axolotl to breathe and protects it from infection.

SWISHING TAIL

The tail is used to propel an axolotl through the water.

GRIPPY TOES

An axolotl's feet help it to grasp rocks and crawl around. There are four toes on each forelimb and five on each hindlimb.

HOW CAN YOU TELL A MALE FROM A FEMALE?

You have to look behind the legs to spot the best way to tell a male from a female. Here you will find the cloaca. The male cloaca is long and bulbous, while the female cloaca is a small bump.

Male

Cloaca

Female

Let's take a closer look at the anatomy of an axolotl. Every part of this underwater creature's body is perfect for what it needs to do—swim, crawl, breathe, eat, sense the world, reproduce, and more!

UNDER THE SKIN

Axolotls are vertebrates, which means they have spines like us. The bones in their limbs look a lot like our own bones. The axolotl's skull protects its brain, and its jaw hinges open to snatch up prey.

FEATHERY GILLS

Part of an axolotl's charm comes from its feathery gills. These are loaded with tiny blood vessels that absorb oxygen from the water so the axolotl can breathe.

MUTANTS

LEUCISTIC

Also known as "white mutants," these are the kind of axolotls most commonly studied by scientists in laboratories. They're also the ones you've probably seen online!

WHITE ALBINO

The color of an axolotl comes from pigments in its skin. White albinos don't have the dark pigment that wild axolotls have. They also have red eyes.

GOLDEN ALBINO

This axolotl also can't produce dark pigment. Instead it has a golden-yellow color.

In the wild, axolotls are a brownish-black color with darker, mottled markings. However, there are many types of axolotl that have mutated and as a result come in all sorts of wonderful colors! Let's meet the mutants.

BLACK MELANOID

Black melanoid axolotls have lots of the black pigment found in wild axolotls but less of the brown pigment, so they are much darker!

COPPER

Copper axolotls look a bit like a mix between leucistic axolotls and wild axolotls.

PIEBALD

A piebald looks like a white axolotl, except it has very dark streaks of pigment creeping down the sides of its body.

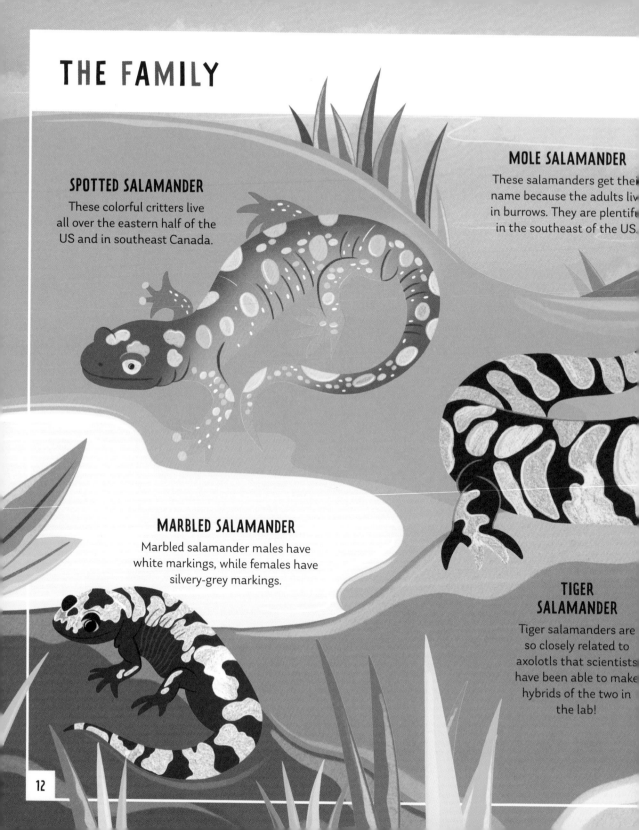

THE FAMILY

SPOTTED SALAMANDER
These colorful critters live all over the eastern half of the US and in southeast Canada.

MOLE SALAMANDER
These salamanders get the name because the adults live in burrows. They are plentiful in the southeast of the US.

MARBLED SALAMANDER
Marbled salamander males have white markings, while females have silvery-grey markings.

TIGER SALAMANDER
Tiger salamanders are so closely related to axolotls that scientists have been able to make hybrids of the two in the lab!

Axolotls belong to the Ambystomatidae family of salamanders. There are two separate parts of this family: Dicamptodon (Pacific giant salamanders) and Ambystoma (which contains the axolotl). The species pictured below are some of the axolotl's closest cousins!

RINGED SALAMANDER

Head to the Ozark Mountains in the US if you want to catch a glimpse of a ringed salamander.

SMALL-MOUTHED SALAMANDER

Sometimes called the Texas salamander, this salamander can live in many US states outside of Texas, including those around the Great Lakes.

A DAY IN THE LIFE

Everyone knows axolotls are super cute, but they're also wild animals, which means every day brings new challenges. From eating to avoiding being eaten, let's have a look at some of their daily activities.

HIDING AMONG PLANTS

The kinds of water-loving plants found in the axolotl habitat include floating primrose-willow, water lettuce, water lilies, water hyacinth, and cattail. Axolotls like to hide out among the plants during the day.

SWIMMING

As a member of the salamander family, axolotls are well-adapted to life underwater. They are good swimmers, in part because they have a strong tail and tailfin.

EATING

Axolotls mostly eat other animals such as sea shrimp and crayfish (which are small crustaceans), insects (especially young insects, called larvae), and small fish. Plants have also been found in their digestive systems, so although they are mostly carnivores (meat-eaters), they sometimes crave some greens!

CREATURES OF THE NIGHT

When the moon and the stars are out, it's axolotl party time! They are nocturnal creatures, meaning they are more active once the sun goes down.

AVOIDING PREDATORS

In the wild, the typical predators axolotls need to watch out for are water snakes and birds. In recent years, however, new predators have been introduced, including carp and tilapia—two kinds of big fish.

LIFE CYCLE

1 **MEET THE PARENTS**
To make an axolotl baby you first need a male and a female to mate. They do this in an unusual way— see pages 18–19 for more details!

2 **EGG-CELLENT IDEA**
After mating, the female lays her eggs on plant leaves, attaching them with sticky mucus. She can lay hundreds at a time!

3 **JELLY BABIES**
For about 10–14 days, the eggs develop in jelly coats. Internal organs are formed, and the babies start to resemble tiny salamanders. The jelly coats protect the young axolotls from infection.

When other salamanders grow up they lose their gills and tails and begin to breathe air, so they can live on land. Axolotls never undergo this change, known as metamorphosis, and as a result spend their lives underwater. Like Peter Pan, they never grow up!

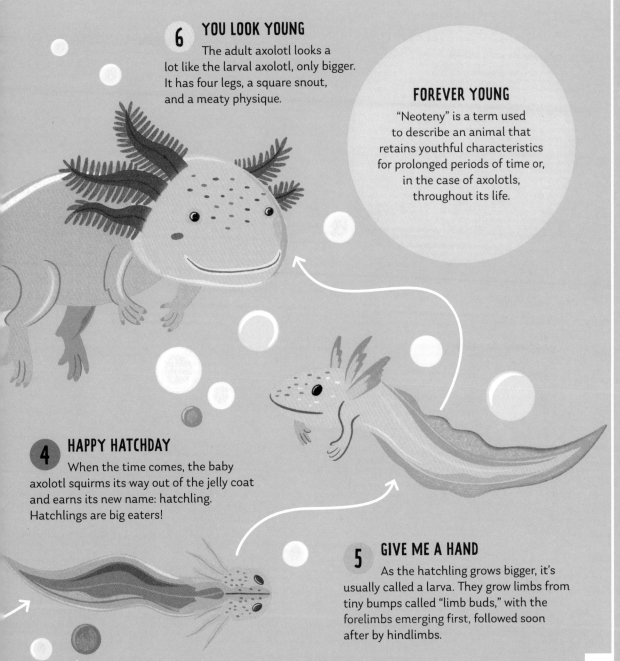

6 YOU LOOK YOUNG

The adult axolotl looks a lot like the larval axolotl, only bigger. It has four legs, a square snout, and a meaty physique.

FOREVER YOUNG

"Neoteny" is a term used to describe an animal that retains youthful characteristics for prolonged periods of time or, in the case of axolotls, throughout its life.

4 HAPPY HATCHDAY

When the time comes, the baby axolotl squirms its way out of the jelly coat and earns its new name: hatchling. Hatchlings are big eaters!

5 GIVE ME A HAND

As the hatchling grows bigger, it's usually called a larva. They grow limbs from tiny bumps called "limb buds," with the forelimbs emerging first, followed soon after by hindlimbs.

DANCE OF THE AXOLOTLS

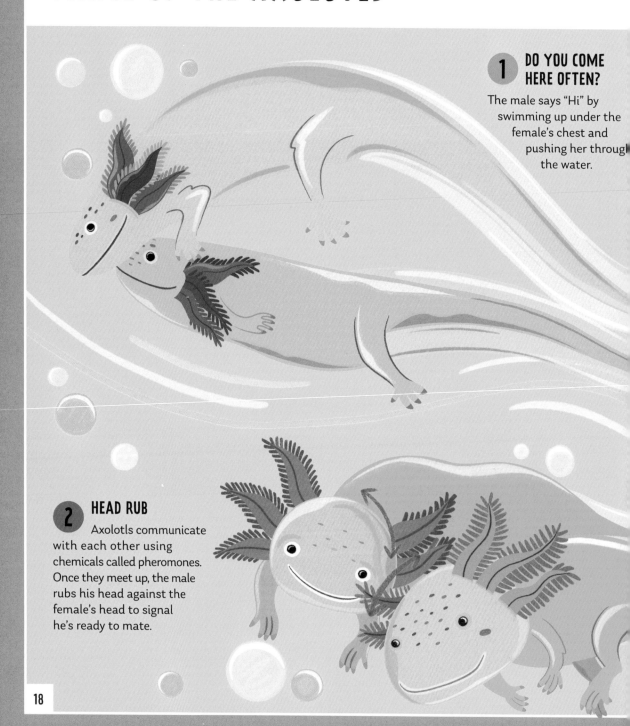

1 DO YOU COME HERE OFTEN?

The male says "Hi" by swimming up under the female's chest and pushing her throug[h] the water.

2 HEAD RUB

Axolotls communicate with each other using chemicals called pheromones. Once they meet up, the male rubs his head against the female's head to signal he's ready to mate.

To make a baby axolotl, a male and a female axolotl have to work together as a team. Like all great love stories, it starts with a dance. Unlike all great love stories, it also involves a lump of jelly on a rock.

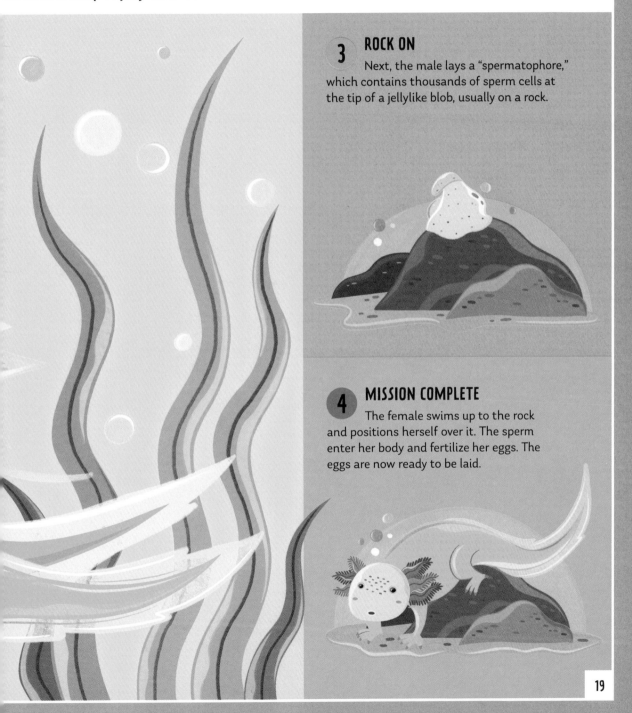

3 ROCK ON

Next, the male lays a "spermatophore," which contains thousands of sperm cells at the tip of a jellylike blob, usually on a rock.

4 MISSION COMPLETE

The female swims up to the rock and positions herself over it. The sperm enter her body and fertilize her eggs. The eggs are now ready to be laid.

SUPERPOWERS

Axolotls have a superpower: they can regrow parts of their bodies after an injury! These amazing amphibians are capable of regenerating limbs, tails, and even sections of their hearts and brains.

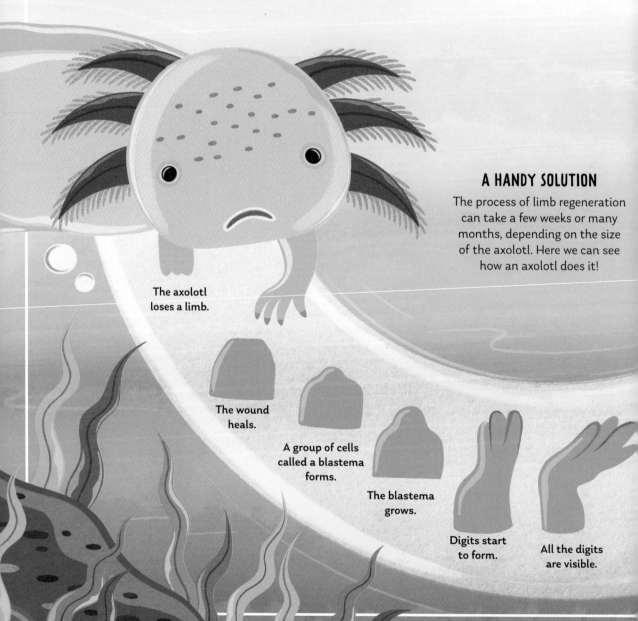

A HANDY SOLUTION

The process of limb regeneration can take a few weeks or many months, depending on the size of the axolotl. Here we can see how an axolotl does it!

The axolotl loses a limb.

The wound heals.

A group of cells called a blastema forms.

The blastema grows.

Digits start to form.

All the digits are visible.

The process is complete!

The limb grows to the correct size.

Reindeer antlers

Starfish

Spiny Mouse

REGENERATORS

While most mammals—including humans—can only regenerate small bits of tissue, other animals are much better regenerators. Male deer shed antlers every year and regenerate them the following year. Starfish, which are invertebrates, can regenerate lost arms, and spiny mice can perfectly regenerate their skin!

HELPING HUMANS

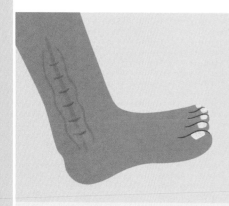

SCARRING

Every time we get a cut, we get a scar. Scars can make it hard for skin to stretch and do all of its jobs. Axolotls usually don't form scars after injuries, and they might hold some good clues for how to help humans heal with less scarring.

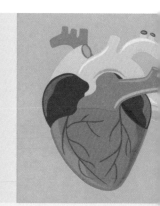

AMPUTEES

Millions of people have lost arms or legs due to injury or disease. Clues for how to regenerate limbs might come from axolotls, and maybe one day this knowledge can help amputees regenerate limbs themselves.

Did you know axolotls might be able to help humans in the future? Scientists who study regeneration in axolotls hope that what they learn might be able to help people who have been injured or who have diseases.

HEART DISEASE

Heart disease causes cells to die and create scar tissue. Perhaps the way axolotls regenerate heart cells could be used to help doctors trying to fight heart disease in humans?

SPINAL CORD INJURY

An axolotl can perfectly repair an injured spinal cord, but human spinal cord injuries can leave a person paralyzed. Understanding how axolotls regenerate spinal cord might help devise treatments for human patients who are unable to move parts of their body.

THREATS AND CONSERVATION

POLLUTION

Pollution from factories, harmful pesticides, and farming fertilizers has made its way into Lake Xochimilco and the connected canals where axolotls live. Axolotls, like other amphibians, are very sensitive to chemicals because they breathe through their skin.

INVASIVE SPECIES

Invasive species are ones that are not native to a region and have usually been introduced by humans. In their habitat, axolotls are now eaten by bigger, invasive fish, which especially love to eat axolotl eggs.

In the wild, axolotls are critically endangered. Their numbers have dwindled in the last few decades, and the main causes are pollution and the introduction of invasive species to their habitat. Conservationists are working hard to protect this precious species.

CONSERVATION EFFORTS

To help axolotls, some farmers are switching to alternative ways of controlling pests and weeds that don't rely on chemicals. Conservationists have created axolotl refuges, where axolotls can live and breed in protected spots. Some are also releasing axolotls bred in captivity into their native habitats, tagging them with microchips to track their fate.

AZTEC ICONS

The Aztecs were people who lived in central and southern Mexico several hundred years ago. The Aztec empire featured sophisticated farming, language, and political systems, as well as unique religious beliefs. The Aztecs lived alongside axolotls, and, as a result, these cute amphibians appear in a lot of Aztec history and mythology.

XOLOTL

Xolotl was the Aztec god of fire and lightning.
To save himself from being sacrificed, he turned
himself into an axolotl! He was the twin of
Quetzalcoatl, the feathered snake god believed
to have created the world. In the Nahuatl
language, axolotl means "water dog" or "water
monster." Axolotls were revered animals and
were featured in mythology and art. They were
also a local food source for humans when they
were plentiful, often served inside tamales
(a dish made from corn dough).

AXOLOTLS TODAY

VIDEO GAMES

Axolotls appear in a lot of computer games. It's not surprising—they look like a video-game character in real life!

CLOTHES AND COSTUMES

If you wanted to dress up as an axolotl for Halloween many years ago, you would have needed a sewing machine! These days, though, you can order up an axolotl costume and have it delivered right to your door.

Nowadays, people can't get enough of these adorable, amazing creatures. However, we must not forget axolotls are endangered animals. Luckily the axolotl's rise in popularity has fueled new interest in helping preserve the species in the wild.

TEDDIES

Do you have an axolotl teddy? Stuffed axolotls can be very cute, and, unlike a real axolotl, you can snuggle this kind in bed!

MONEY

The 50-peso Mexican banknote features an axolotl frolicking among ahuejote trees in chinampas—floating farms in the canals and swamps of Lake Xochimilco.

SCIENCE MUSEUMS AND ZOOS

Many zoos have an axolotl on display, so check out the one nearest to you if you want to see one for yourself. Some science museums also have axolotl exhibitions, where you can learn more about axolotls and maybe even meet an axolotl expert.

GLOSSARY

Amphibian
A type of animal that typically spends some of its life in water and some on land. Frogs, newts, and salamanders are amphibians.

Biologist
A scientist who studies the living world.

Blastema
A bump that forms on the stump of a lost axolotl limb that contains the cells used to grow a new limb.

Chinampas
Floating islands made by humans used to grow crops in Lake Xochimilco in Mexico.

Carnivore
A meat-eater.

Conservationist
A person who works to protect the natural world.

DNA
Information contained in the cells of all living things that determines how they look and function.

Gills
The frilly parts flanking both sides of the axolotl head used for absorbing oxygen from the water into its blood.

Invertebrate
An animal without a backbone, for example an insect.

Jelly coat
The clear slime layer that covers and protects axolotl eggs.

Metamorphosis
The process of an animal changing from one state to another, for example a tadpole to a frog. Many salamanders undergo metamorphosis before leaving the water so they can live on land.

Mutant
An animal that has a different trait from other animals of the same species because of a mutation (change) in its DNA.

Regeneration
The process of growing again. In biology, it often refers to how a creature restores part of its body after injury or disease.

Spermatophore
A gooey packet of jellylike material that contains axolotl sperm and is usually stuck to a rock.

Vertebrate
An animal with a spine, for example an axolotl.

Xochimilco
A lake near Mexico City, Mexico, where axolotls live.

Xolotl
The Aztec god of fire and lightning who turned himself into an axolotl to avoid being sacrificed.

INDEX

Ambystoma 13
Ambystomatidae 5, 13
amphibians 5
amputees 22
biologists 4
blastemas 20
bones 9, 23
brains 9, 20
cameras 7
carnivores 15
carp 15
chinampas 29
cloacas 8
computers 7
conservation 24–25
conservationists 25
crayfish 15
crustaceans 5
deer 21
Dicamptodon 13
DNA 7
eggs 16, 24
factories 24
farmers 25
Aztecs 26–27
fish 5, 15, 24
gills 9, 17
Harvard University 4
hatchlings 17
heart disease 23
hearts 20, 23
insect repellent 6
insects 5, 6, 15
invasive species 24
invertebrates 21
jelly coats 16
Lake Chalco 5, 7
Lake Xochimilco 5, 7, 24
life cycles 16–17
limbs 4, 8, 20–21

marbled salamanders 12
mating 16, 18–19
metamorphosis 17
microscopes 7
mole salamanders 12
money 29
museums 29
mutants 10–11
neoteny 17
notebooks 6
pencils 6
pens 6
pheromones 18
pollution 24–25
predators 15
Quetzalcoatl (Aztec god) 27
regeneration 20–21
ringed salamanders 13
salamanders 5, 12–13, 17
sea shrimp 15
skeletons 9
skin 8
small-mouthed salamanders 13
snakes 15
spermatophores 19
spiny mice 21
spotted salamanders 12
starfish 21
sunscreen 6
tadpoles 5
tails 8, 14, 20
tamales 27
tiger salamanders 12
tilapia 15
toes 8
vertebrates 9
video games 28
worms 5
Xolotl (Aztec god) 27
zoos 29

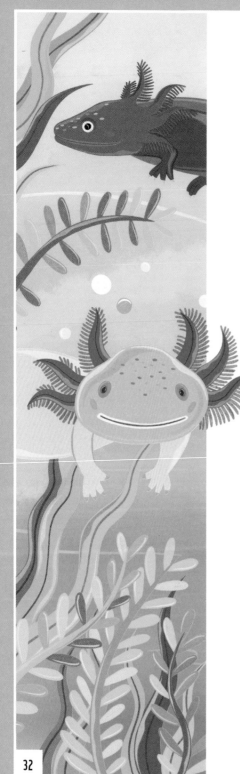

This has been a

NEON ✦ SQUID

production

Dedicated with love to Ashton and Oakley

Author: Dr. Jessica LaMae Whited
Illustrator: Bethany Lord

Design: Collaborate Agency
US Editor: Jill Freshney
Proofreader: Joseph Barnes

Copyright © 2024
St. Martin's Press
120 Broadway, New York,
NY 10271

Created for St. Martin's Press
by Neon Squid
The Smithson, 6 Briset Street,
London, EC1M 5NR

EU representative: Macmillan
Publishers Ireland Ltd,
1st Floor, The Liffey Trust Centre,
117–126 Sheriff Street Upper,
Dublin 1, D01 YC43

10 9 8 7 6 5 4 3 2 1

Library of Congress Cataloging-
in-Publication Data is available.

Printed and bound in
Guangdong, China by
Leo Paper Products Ltd.

ISBN: 978-1-684-49511-5

Published in October 2024.

www.neonsquidbooks.com

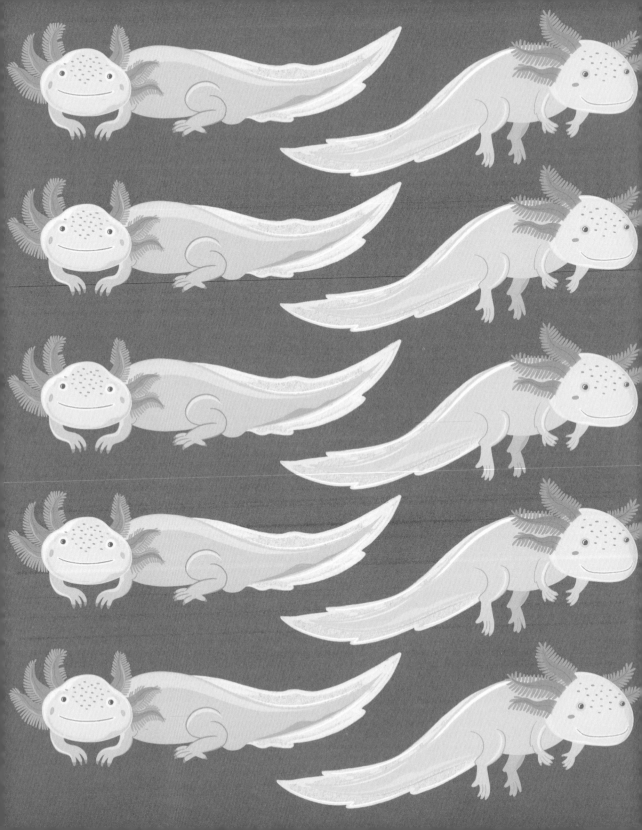